"Thatcher's Way"

Watercolour Painting Simplified

with

Bryan A. Thatcher. The "Wet-into-Wet" artist, author and tutor

Published by Windsor & Peacock

Cover Picture:

"Boats at Hastings" Reproduced as a demonstration
on page 34

"Watercolour Painting Simplified"
Published to coincide with the production of the
VHS Video of the same title. Available firect from
the author.

Other VHS Video Tapes titles available:

1. Wet-into-Wet
2. More Wet-into-Wet
3. Landscapes & Trees Wet-into-Wet
4. Paint Flowers Wet-into-Wet

Bryan A. Thatcher
The Studio
168 Pinner Road
Watford Heath
England
Herts WD1 4EW
Tel: 01923 227177

Printed by The Manson Group Limited, St. Albans

Dedications

&

ACKNOWLEDGEMENTS

I shall always be grateful to my parents, who gave me great encouragement in all things, especially the benefit of their own happiness. To my wife Denise for her patients (!) and help with my spelling! Also to my friend Dr. Hans Patel, without his help this book would never have happened.

**Windsor & Peacock
Publishers**

14 South Approach
Moor Park Northwood
Middlesex HA6 2ET
England

Telephone: +44 (0)1923 836064
Fax : +44 (0)1923 836063

ISBN NUMBER: 0-9537985-0-X

Contents

Foreword by Jan Leeming

Artistically, it was my lucky day when I met Bryan Thatcher. All my life I have been drawn to the Creative Arts and even thought about having a go at painting. I did nothing about it until my dear friend Chlöe phoned to say she'd booked us in for Adult Education Classes in the Art of Drawing and Watercolour. We dutifully attended classes for two years but weren't really getting anywhere – our work was stiff, unimaginative – almost painting by numbers. Then I met Bryan and greatly admired his loose flowing style and wonderful skies, which I didn't think for one moment I could emulate. I've never been taught to draw and didn't take Art as an exam subject at school. Bryan threw out a challenge that if I attended a class, I'd walk away after two hours with a painting that I liked and was pleased with.

I roped in Chlöe and off we set for his studio near Watford. I've stillgot the work – a simple windmill in a field – to remind me of that wonderful breakthrough when Chlöe and I felt Bryan had opened the door for us onto the immensely satisfying world of painting. Over many courses and many years, I've watched Bryan wave his magic paintbrush over so many folk – helping, encouraging and always improving. He is an exceptionally good teacher with kind works for all. He doesn't blind you with science and is quite happy to share his 'cheats' with us – easy ways of doing things to get an end result. I've never heard him put a student down or say anything negative – if it doesn't seem to be working he will find a way of turning the 'mistakes' into positives.

Last year, I moved home and am now so far away that I can only get back for the occasional class. I miss them very much. But now with 'Book Title' beside me, I shall look forward to many more hours of painting with Bryan. His new book is written in such a straightforward, no nonsense way, anyone with some knowledge of watercolour painting will be able to follow it. The only trouble is I won't hear him saying – 'don't put a wet brush into a damp colour' and 'don't fiddle'.

The Author

Introduction

I am particularly pleased to be putting pen to paper again. My previous book, "Wet-into-Wet", was my first publication and has been extremely popular. This book is a little more adventurous in that I have included quite a number of my more recent works – and have done my best to explain how I painted them.

I have been much encouraged to produce this new book. Not least of all by the many followers I have been fortunate to meet when tutoring watercolour painting courses throughout the UK, Europe and in the USA. Our wonderful world of "Picture Making" is a pastime enjoyed by many pleasant people, a great many of whom are very modest about their obvious talent. If I have helped one or two of them, I am very pleased.

When I am not painting I play some golf. It was on the golf course that I first met Dr. Hans Patel. Hans and his wife Paru have since joined my army of students – and are now producing some very fine work. It is he who is partly responsible for this book, and he is now my publisher. We still play golf together and have become firm friends.

Jan Leeming has been kind enough to add a few kind words for me. Jan and I met some few years ago when I was exhibiting some of my work near her home, at the time, in Buckinghamshire. She is extremely talented in several crafts and is a watercolourist who I would describe as well above average. While being busy with her television work, she still finds time to paint and has regularly attended my courses.

There are many styles and different ways of expressing one's work in Watercolour. I am sure that is what makes painting such a challenge. We all like to be different, and no doubt we are. Once the basics are in place we can experiment with all kinds of techniques. My work has been described as loose, original and fiddle free. I take that as a compliment. My main aim is to be free of unnecessary detail, with an emphasis on loose brush strokes combining with attractive washes laid wet-into-wet. This does help to give a transparent result. A good test of a true conventional watercolour is to be able to see the paper through the colour.

I hope you enjoy this book, that it may give you ideas for you own work and above all I hope that if you have attended any of my watercolour coursed you are able to say, "I wondered how he did that, now I know, it looks so easy."

 "Happy Painting" to you all.

MY MATERIALS

I believe there is an opinion that, of all painting mediums, watercolour is the most difficult to master. Well, let me tell you that we never master it! The watercolour medium has a mind of it's very own. Tell it what to do and it will not be your friend. We will reap the benefits of this beautiful medium if we accept what it offers us – and above all, whatever you do, do not fiddle. I sometimes mention when tutoring my students that a good watercolour is not finished until it is ruined! Many a true word spoken in jest!

There are however quite a few things we can do to help reduce the number of "disasters". The first is undoubtedly the use of the very best materials one can sensibly afford. The use of unsuitable paper, brushes and too many colours are three areas that will almost certainly cause problems.

So let me tell you about my materials.

Paper

I believe that the paper we use is possibly the most important of all our materials. Imagine painting a masterpiece on a paper that will disintegrate within a year or two! I thoroughly recommend the use of a fairly heavyweight rag content purpose made watercolour paper. I use 200lb (approx. 425grm) and 300lb (approx. 600grm) rough surface papers. At these weights there is no need for stretching – an operation which I consider to be a waste of good painting time. I prefer a Rough surface to a Hot Pressed or Not surface as this offers more options, particularly when a dry brush technique is required.

Heavier paper is more expensive than a 90lb or 140lb paper but I find it well worth the extra cost. It is best to buy paper from a merchant rather than the art store, quite a saving can be made. The brand names of the paper that I have used for the paintings in this book are Whatman and Saunders Waterford.

I find that rag-content watercolour paper is preferable to a wood pulp paper. The colour appears to sit on the surface more happily. Having said that, I use a wood pulp paper, such as Bockingford, for pen and pencil sketching. If the cheaper brands of paper are not sized correctly they can absorb the colour like blotting paper – so be warned.

Colours – Tubes or Pans

I have always used tube colours. I use a watercolour box with several sections, which I continually refill. Pan colours are generally not large enough for my large brushes and I also fine that tube colours remain moist much longer.

But what about the choice of colours? This is of course a personal matter, but it is essential to recognise that we do not buy a colour for its appearance. We need to understand – by practise and experimentation – what it will do when mixed with the other colours in our palette.

Colours. Tubes or Pans (Cont.)

Most of the colour manufacturers have around eighty colours in their range. Do not be tempted to buy too many, about a dozen will be sufficient for most of us. It is best to include two reds, two yellows and two blues, plus something like a neutral tint. Just twelve colours will give you the opportunity to mix a great many hues, tints and greys. This can be very rewarding if you have the time to practice – as long as you make written notes of how you mixed the tints – otherwise you will have to have a mastermind to remember them!

Sticking to a limited palette, you will learn to mix colours that will help your work to be easily recognised as "Your style."

The tube colours I use regularly are:

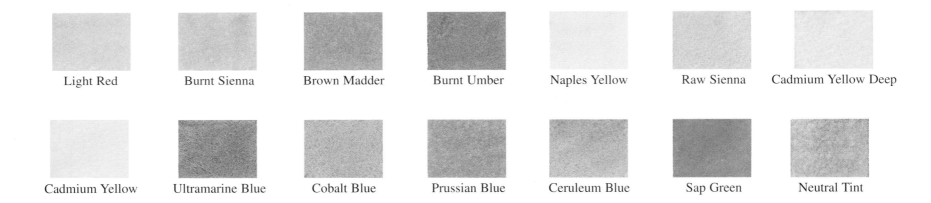

| Light Red | Burnt Sienna | Brown Madder | Burnt Umber | Naples Yellow | Raw Sienna | Cadmium Yellow Deep |

| Cadmium Yellow | Ultramarine Blue | Cobalt Blue | Prussian Blue | Ceruleum Blue | Sap Green | Neutral Tint |

*I occasionally add a new colour to experiment with, but the above colours have been my main palette for many years.

Some useful colour mixes

The following colour mixes have been made from some of the colours in my palette. You may find them useful.

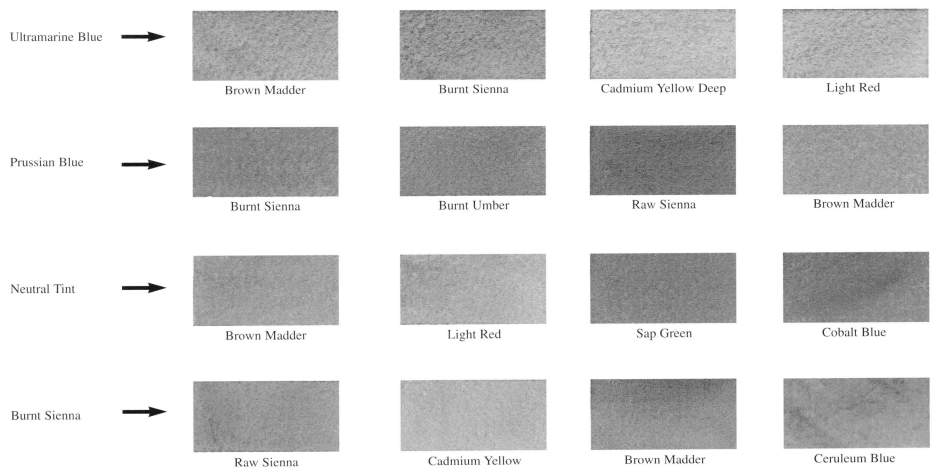

Ultramarine Blue →	Brown Madder	Burnt Sienna	Cadmium Yellow Deep	Light Red
Prussian Blue →	Burnt Sienna	Burnt Umber	Raw Sienna	Brown Madder
Neutral Tint →	Brown Madder	Light Red	Sap Green	Cobalt Blue
Burnt Sienna →	Raw Sienna	Cadmium Yellow	Brown Madder	Ceruleum Blue

* You will undoubtedly find all kinds of greys in the corners of your palette. Don''t forget to try them before washing them away!

Brushes

When tutoring my courses, I see students (fellow artists) unloading their equipment on arrival at the venue and I never cease to be amazed at the number of brushes some of them have acquired. It is so easy to be tempted to buy new equipment in the art store – which must appear to be an Aladdin's Cave to enthusiastic newcomers in our wonderful world of picture making.

It is actually quite surprising how few brushes we need. The brushes I use regularly are pictured below.

Large Wash Brush   I prefer a Flat Hogs Hair 1½ inches wide.

Size 4, 6, 8, 10, 12 & 14 Round Sables   I have Kolinsky sables, but a good quality mixture of synthetic & sable is good value.

No 3 Rigger   This is useful for trees, foliage and subtle darks etc.

One inch and a two inch Chisel edge   The synthetic variety are just right for masts on boats and telegraph poles etc.

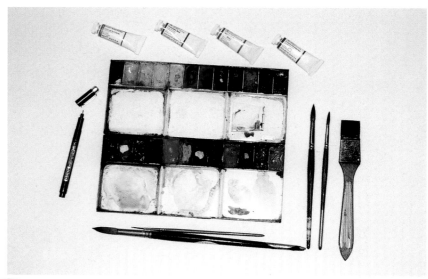

Sundry Materials

In addition to our paper, colours and brushes, there are a number of other items that we need from time to time.

These extra materials will depend of course on whether we are painting out on location, or in the comfort of a studio. It's all too easy to take more than we need and in any event we really do have to leave room for that thermos flask of tea!

Here is a list of my extras.

Sketch book and range of pencils	Absolutely invaluable.
Waterproof drawing pen	Useful for quick line drawings
Roll of tissues	Numerous uses – clearing excess moisture etc.
Small sponge and putty rubber	For lifting colour out
Scissors	Trimming large sheets
Stool	More comfortable than grass!
Easel	I prefer a lightweight metal easel with varying height adjustments
Small groundsheet	Laid around my easel, it catches all I drop.
Painting board	Plywood, approx 24" x 18".
Pencils	2b and 4b – and a putty rubber.

All my materials are kept in my estate car – and I do confess to parking quite close to my painting area!

Those all important sketches

Here are one or two sketches, which I've found helpful to make when planning a composition. These I make either in my sketch book , or in some cases on a sheet of "Not" surface watercolour paper. One can produce several of these in a short period of time and then return to the studio to paint more serious work from them. The advantage of painting from sketches is that one can leave out unwanted detail and so not be tempted to include it if it is not in the sketch!

2b pencil on Light Red Wash

2b pencil and Watercolours

Watercolour sketch

Watercolour sketch

The Value of Thumbnail Sketches

Before launching into a "Masterpiece," it is sometimes worth considering a small "Thumbnail sketch" of the subject you have in mind. This helps to get to know the subject, plan the composition and to consider the colours to be used. This page illustrates a sheet from my sketchbook. On location in Ireland, in the beautiful Co. Clare, these sketches were painted as small demonstrations. Much better to return home from a painting course with a few of these – rather than a roll of film, which can never catch the atmosphere we feel.

Grey Limestone Rocks on the beach
at Doolin, Co. Clare.

Cliffs of Moher (1) from Doolin.

Cliffs of Moher (2) from Doolin.

* I used masking tape to give me the crisp edges around each sketch.

More Sketches

Cottage at Bishops Quarter, Co. Clare

Cottage on The Burren, Co. Clare

Boats at Bishops Quarter, Co. Clare

Woodland Stream

These watercolour sketches were made in Ireland and will be useful for future paintings.

More Sketches

Pen and Wash. Corfu.

Watercolour sketch in Co. Clare, Ireland.

2b Pencil sketch in Cumbria

Watercolour sketch in Cadiz. Spain.

* Most of my sketching is done with a brush and watercolours, although I do make a pencil sketch occasionally.

Painting Trees

I believe I once heard it said that if you can paint a tree then you can paint a landscape. Well, I am not too sure about that, but it certainly helps. Trees of course, come in all shapes and sizes, and just as importantly in many differing colours. We all admire those wonderful autumn colours. If you are like me you cannot wait to get your brushes out when September arrives! I am probably biased, but as artists we perhaps appreciate those colours far more than most folk.

Note the "Bird Holes"

I try to visualise the overall shape of a tree, or clump of trees, before putting brush to paper. I actually half close my eyes – this seems to cut out some of the detail and one can get a better idea of that all important overall shape.

Using a rough surface paper helps a dry brush effect to leave "bird holes" – into which branches can be indicated with a Rigger brush.

The small demonstration tree formation on the left shows branches added to the bird holes. The tree trunks were also added after the foliage was painted. The green was made from a mix of Raw Sienna and Prussian Blue.

A group of trees seem to work better as they will overlap each other and therefore form an interesting overall shape. A single tree does tend to look lonely, but this can be helped with the addition of surrounding bushes and undergrowth.

Mixing greens is important to us when painting trees – best not to use too many manufactured greens. Here are a few mixes which you might find helpful..

Raw Sienna and Prussian Blue.

Raw Sienna and Ultramarine Blue.

Raw Sienna and Cobalt Blue.

Cadmium Yellow Deep
& Ultramarine Blue.

Burnt Sienna and Prussian Blue.

Burnt Umber and Prussian Blue.

Tree Studies

Pine Trees. See page 66.

Winter Trees. See page 64.

Palm Trees.

Bluebell Wood. See page 68.

Painting Boats

Here are a few simple examples of painting boats in watercolour. When painting boats it is as well to remember that we have "Artistic License."In a busy harbour you may well find a huge number of differing crafts. Some can be quite complicated in their structure and character. Select the ones that you can comfortably cope with in your painting. Take sketches, or even photographs of some of the more demanding boats, these can be a useful reference for future paintings.

Four separate "Quickies" – ideal for future reference.

More Boats

The initial overall wash has added atmosphere here.

The drama in the sky, made from Naples Yellow and Light Red, seems to be the focal point here.

More Boats

These lovely old barges always make a good composition.

An overall initial wash of Light Red and Cobalt Blue make both of these paintings into quite a reasonable pair.

More Boats

Contrasting colours have been used here. It is unusual to have a warm distance and a cool foreground , but it seems to work.

Boats in the seascape here. The blue in the sky acts as an interesting foil.

Painting Snow

Painting snow in watercolour is perhaps ideal for newcomers to the medium – as long as one is not sitting out in a snowdrift! In the winter months a subject can be taken from the sketchbook, or maybe a photograph can be used as a reference, and the painting can be done in the comfort of the studio.

The white of the paper can be used for most of the snow – so the painting is almost half done before you begin! Here are a couple of examples, of which one is somewhat different. The snowflakes were made by dropping crystals of salt on to damp washes. The wetter the washes, the larger the flakes. Likewise the less wet washes will give smaller flakes. Using salt can be quite an interesting experiment for all kinds of effects.

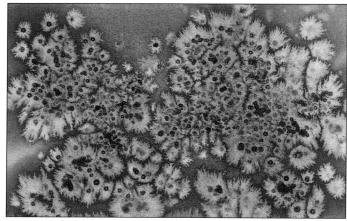

After the salt was added, I dropped various colours on to the salt crystals and just let them react.

The contrast of white snow, combined with a few strong tones will always help the aerial perspective of a painting.

Painting Snow

Adding just a touch of warmth can help a snow scene. Light Red was used here on the hill and in the foreground.

Painting Snow

Adding just a touch of warmth can help a snow scene. Light Red was used here on the hill and in the foreground.

Figures – In The Landscape

There is no doubt that our landscape and townscape paintings can be greatly enhanced and carry much more interest when figures are included. It helps to understand that these figures need not be of a portrait nature. Just an indication of a figure will suffice.

Here are a few examples, which you may find helpful.

These figures are really just brush strokes. No necks and no feet! The heads should not be too round – and have you noticed how the grey figures, in the bottom right hand sketch, appear to be further away? Their heads are at a similar level too.

More Figures in the Landscape

FIGURES ON
THE BEACH.
JERSEY 8/98

This is a page from my sketchbook. These were all painted on various beaches on Jersey. Note how simple the figures are.

More Figures in the Landscape

A cloudy day in Jersey – but the figures add interest to the atmosphere.

A warmer atmosphere here and the simple figures again help the subject.

More Figures – In The Landscape

Even the presence of small figures will add life to our paintings! Both these fifteen minute sketches were made in Jersey.

More Figures in the Landscape

This chap had no luck while I was sketching him. We did however, have an interesting conversation about his own watercolour painting. Yes, he did paint "Wet-into-Wet."

This small watercolour made quite a nice Christmas card some while ago.

More Figures – In The Landscape

A small village square in the South of France – and two lonely figures waiting for the doors to open!

Market day in a town quite close to Toulouse in France. A demonstration while tutoring there in 1996.

More Figures – In The Landscape

The figures in a painting do not have to be human! These chickens were just a few of many at Shinafoot Farm in Perthshire, Scotland.

Corfe Castle in Dorset is usually busier than this. Could do with a few more figures here.

Calf Close Bay, Detail.

Calf Close Bay, Derwentwater

With materials at hand and washes ready mixed, this small watercolour can be sketched in a little more fifteen minutes. It is quite an interesting exercise to sometimes fix a time on this type of work. It really is quite surprising how little time it can take.

Ready mixed washes required are:

1. Cobalt Blue and Neutral Tint   2. Light Red   3. Sap Green   4 Burnt Sienna

A size ten Round Sable and a sketchbook are all that one requires.

This was painted as a reference sketch so I decided that a sky was not required on this occasion. I was able to proceed straight away with the hills. The four hills were painted as one overall shape with the grey wash of Cobalt Blue and Neutral Tint. With the hills still wet, I ran Sap Green into the hill on the left and Light Red into the hill on the right. I also softened the top of the distant hills by wiping their top edges with a clean tissue.

When the two main hills were just damp, I indicated the trees with a mix of Sap Green and Neutral Tint. When painting into a damp colour, it is essential that the brush is not too wet – otherwise a drying stain will result. These stains are sometimes referred to as "cauliflowers."

I repeated all these colours in the foreground lake, and added the bank on the left with Burnt Sienna. The darker tones on the lake and bank were just Neutral Tint. Note that I retained some of the white paper to give contrast.

* When painting into a damp colour it is essential that ones' brush is not too wet. Otherwise a drying stain (Cauliflower) may result.

A typical "Wet-into-Wet" Watercolour Sketch

This is typical of the type of watercolour sketches that I really enjoy producing. This will have taken no more than fifteen minutes to paint using a single round sable on a Whatman Watercolour Block.

The location is at Calf Close Bay on Derwentwater, quite near Keswick in Cumbria. My fellow painters on this painting course, based at nearby Higham Hall, all produced this subject fairly quickly. No fiddling here, as you can see, no real detail, just broad brush strokes indicating the main shapes.

The middle distance (The Gateway to Borrowdale) is painted in a cool grey, (Cobalt Blue and Neutral Tint), and the foreground is warm with Burnt Sienna. All colours painted "Wet-into- Wet" or "Damp into damp."

* If you sometimes find Drying Stains, sometimes referred to as "Cauliflowers", creeping into your work, try to resist painting "Wet-into-Damp."

Boats at Hastings, Detail.

Boats at Hastings

A harbour full of boats has long been a favourite subject of mine. The masts reaching up into the sky always help with the composition and the differing shapes are always a challenge. The Old Town at Hastings in Sussex is always worth a visit and still holds much of the charm of years gone by. Much to paint here, but on this occasion I settled for these lovely old boats.

Colours used here are:

Naples Yellow, Light Red, Ultramarine Blue, Brown Madder, Neutral Tint, and Burnt Sienna.

I used a size ten Round Sable, a Rigger and my large flat Wash Brush on Whatman 200lb rough surface paper size 11" x 15."

I did no drawing here, although I had sketched the subject in pen and wash to work out a suitable composition. I dampened the sky area with clean water and dropped a weak wash of Naples Yellow into the centre and followed this with just a touch of Light Red, which I ran in from both sides. Whilst still wet, I added a mix of Ultramarine Blue and Brown Madder and allowed the whole painting to dry.

The distant hills were a mixture of Ultramarine Blue and Neutral tint and the building on the extreme right was made with Light Red and Neutral Tint. The main boat, just right of centre, was brushed in with Brown Madder and I added Burnt Sienna for the subtle change of colour. The boats on either side were illustrated Neutral Tint and the boat on the extreme left was made out of Brown Madder on its left and Burnt Sienna on the right lighter side. The remaining posts, boats and cabins were painted firstly with a weak wash of Neutral Tint and the shadows were added a stronger Neutral Tint using my Rigger. I then painted the masts and figures with Brown Madder and Neutral Tint. I also dropped in a touch of neat Brown Madder on the red figure on the right of the painting.

The foreground was a weak wash of Light Red with Neutral Tint being added to make the subtle shadows. When this was dry I added more Neutral Tint with the Rigger to make slightly darker shadows and suggestions of trailing ropes.

* When painting boats it sometimes helps the composition if a number of them overlap each other.

Boats at Hastings

Detail.

The Cliffs of Moher, County Clare, Ireland

I have been tutoring watercolour courses in Ireland for a few years now, and such is the friendliness of this wonderful island, that I look forward to returning each and every time. A short taxi drive from Shannon airport is the Burin Painting Centre in Lisdoonvarna. This is where we are based, and from here we can travel to the beautiful coastline of Galway Bay to the north and the Cliffs of Moher to the south.

Brushes used here were:

Flat wash brush, size ten Round Sable and my Rigger; on Saunders Waterford 300lb rough surface size 11" x 15"

Colours: Naples Yellow, Neutral Tint, Cobalt Blue, Ceruleum Blue, Ultramarine Blue, Brown Madder, Burnt Sienna, Raw Sienna and Cadmium Red.

I dampened the whole of the sky area with a weak wash of Naples Yellow and whilst still wet dropped in Neutral Tint to indicate the subtle cloud formation. I tilted my board to allow the Neutral Tint to run away from the light areas. When completely dry I suggested the distant hill with a mix of Neutral Tint and Cobalt Blue.

The main cliff on the left was first painted with a mixture of Ultramarine Blue and just a little Brown Madder. This blue/grey allowed me to drop Raw Sienna on to the top of the hill to make the green grass. The sides of the cliffs were still damp when I added various strengths of Cobalt Blue and Brown Madder – leaving some of the under colour to show through as lights on the rocks.

Horizontal brush strokes of firstly Ceruleum Blue and a mixture of Cobalt Blue and Neutral Tint made the water – I left the white of the paper to give me the lights, and then dropped in a touch of Naples Yellow to add colour. I then stroked a light wash of Burnt Sienna across the foreground and while still wet I added a thin wash of Neutral Tint across the bottom foreground. The suggestion of darks were added with my Rigger, using a mix of Brown Madder and Neutral Tint. I used artistic licence to add the yacht, I felt that it helped the composition, with just a touch of Cadmium Red.

Naples Yellow can be quite opaque if used too strongly. It can also turn other colours cloudy when mixed in a wash. I use it on it's own – thinly.

Cliffs of Moher. G. Clare.

Bryan A. Thatcher.

The Cliffs of Moher, Co. Clare, Ireland.

Detail of broken edge.

Great Gable on Wastwater, Cumbria

Is there anywhere to match the atmosphere of our own Lake District? I have tutored courses here for many years and look forward each time to returning. There is always a differing sky above those wonderful hills.

Here we are on Wastwater with Great Gable peering down on us. I have added even more light in the sky and I think it has worked quite well.

I have used a size ten sable, a rigger and my large flat wash brush. Whatman 200lb rough paper size 11" x 15".

My colours used here are:

Naples Yellow, Brown Madder, Ultramarine Blue, Raw Sienna, Burnt Sienna, Cadmium Yellow Deep and Neutral Tint.

No pencil drawing here. I dampened the sky area with clean water and dropped Naples Yellow into the central light. While this was still wet, I brushed in from each side of the sky a mixture of Brown Madder and Ultramarine Blue. I tilted my board to encourage this colour to run away from the central light. All these colours were painted with my flat wash brush. This was then allowed to dry thoroughly before proceeding further.

Using my size ten sable, Great Gable, on the left of the landscape, came next. I used a mixture of Brown Madder and Ultramarine Blue to paint the overall shape of this great hill. I then dropped Cadmium Yellow Deep into the top of the hill, and Burnt Sienna into the base. While still damp, I pushed the colour in with my thumb to give the broken light effect to that edge. (See detail above)

The hill on the right was added with a mixture of Raw Sienna, Cadmium Yellow Deep and Ultramarine Blue, ensuring that the bottom of the hill was softened with a clean damp brush. The distant hill was made out of Neutral Tint and I pushed the wet colour back to the right with a clean tissue, which helped to give the impression that the central light was falling in front of the hill.

I repeated the sky colours in the foreground lake, leaving the rough surface of the paper to give me white dry lights as highlights. I kept any strong colour away from the centre of the lake to help the reflected light. Burnt Sienna was added to the top of the lake, the rocks were made with Neutral Tint and Brown Madder, using my rigger brush. A touch of Raw Sienna helped reflect the hills. Job done! Quite a satisfying result.

When painting a subject such as this it really does help if you use your usual colours, – those you know – and do not try to match the actual colours of the landscape in front of you. The camera can do that, but we certainly do not want a photographic result.

* When painting a subject such as this it really does help if you use your usual colours – those you know – and do not try to match the actual colours of the landscape in front of you. The camera can do that, but we certainly do not want a photographic result.

Great Gable, Lake District

Bryan A. Thatcher

Great Gable on Wastwater, Cumbria.

Detail. Galway Bay.

Galway Bay from County Clare

Galway bay has a charm all of it's own. Looking out from the west coast of Ireland the drama in the skies is always a challenge. On this course we decided that a sky study was called for. We had just enjoyed lunch at the Bishops Quarter and, as I recall, even the "locals" on the course could not their brushes out quickly enough.

I used my flat wash brush on the sky, and then a size ten sable and a rigger.

Whatman 200lb rough surface was my choice of paper, nice and white.

The colours used were:

Ultramarine Blue, Brown Madder Light Red, Raw Sienna, Burnt Sienna and Neutral Tint.

I covered the whole of the sky area with a mix of Ultramarine Blue and Brown Madder. While still wet, I dropped in just a touch of weak Light Red in the top right and left hand corners, also just at the horizon on the left. I then allowed these washes to dampen slightly before lifting out the clouds with a clean tissue. Before the sky was completely dry, I added the distant hill with a mix of Ultramarine Blue, weak Brown Madder and a touch of Light Red. I then allowed the painting to dry before any further work was done.

The hill on the right came next. Ultramarine Blue and Brown Madder were mixed together and made the overall shape. I left a few lights so that sky colour was left to indicate lighter rocks, then dropped in a touch of Raw Sienna which made the green grass. I used my Rigger to suggest the darks with Neutral Tint.

The water was made out of Ultramarine Blue and Brown Madder, using a dry brush on dry paper which left lights at the base of the water. The top of the water, nearer the horizon, was darkened with a stronger mix of the two colours together with Burnt Sienna on Rigger to indicate sandy rocks.

Burnt Sienna and Raw Sienna were mixed together for the foreground sandy beach, and when this was dry I added the foreground rocks with my rigger, using first, neat Burnt Sienna then Neutral Tint in varying strengths.

* A subject with a busy sky usually works better with a quiet foreground.

Galway Bay from County Clare.

Detail showing simple figures

Whitesands Bay, Pembrokeshire

On a recent family holiday in Pembrokeshire we stayed at Solva and visited this beach at Whitesands Bay several time during the week. A good subject for painting, the beach was always busy which provided a good opportunity to practice figure painting.

I used a size ten round sable and the small figures, rocks and birds were painted with my rigger. The paper was Saunders Waterford 300lb rough , size 11" x 15."

The colours used were:

Cobalt Blue, Neutral Tint, Raw Sienna, Burnt Sienna, Burnt Umber, Cadmium Red, Ceruleum Blue and Cadmium Orange.

The sky came first with varying strengths of Cobalt Blue. I left some dry white paper for the clouds. The distant hills were a mix of Cobalt Blue and Neutral Tint. Before that had dried, I added the green hill on the left, using Raw Sienna and a touch of Burnt Umber.

The rocks in the distant water and the birds in the sky were indicated with a mix of Burnt Umber and Neutral Tint using my Rigger brush.

I used varying strengths of Cobalt Blue and Ceruleum Blue for the sea – ensuring that my round sable brush strokes were horizontal. I also left some paper to give movement to the water.

The foreground sand is a mix of Raw and Burnt Sienna, leaving a few horizontal lights to add interest.

The figures were painted with my rigger. Note how my figures have no necks and no feet! Various bright colours were used – Cadmium Red, Cadmium Orange, Ceruleum Blue- in addition to Burnt Umber and Neutral Tint. It is a good idea to practice these figures on a sketchpad before committing them to the painting.

* See page 26 for more tips on painting figures.

Whitesands Bay, Pembrokeshire

Autumn Woodland. Detail.

Autumn Woodland

Who can resist painting the wonderful colours we confront in the Autumn months of September and October? Out come those beautiful warm colours that we probably don't use often enough. This small cameo was painted quite close to my home in Hertfordshire. I was out painting on my own – but soon had a few passers-by lingering to see how I was coping. I was rather pleased with the result.

I used my size ten round sable and a rigger on Whatman 200lb rough paper, size 8" x 10".

Colours used were:

Cadmium Orange, Cadmium Red, Cadmium Yellow Deep, Brown Madder, Light Red, Raw Sienna, Neutral Tint and Cobalt Blue.

No drawing was done here, it was straight in with the colours. A weak wash of Cobalt Blue was brushed into the two top corners to give me the sky. (More sky on the left than the right) A touch of Brown Madder and Cobalt Blue painted "Wet-into- Wet" indicated the distant trees just under the sky.

I then painted very loosely, with a dry brush and varying tones of Cadmium Orange , Cadmium Yellow Deep and just a touch of Cadmium Red to indicate the warm "under-colours" of the trees. When these were dry I repeated the same colours with a dry brush to give the effect of some foliage, leaving some of the "under-colour" to show through. I allowed all these colours to dry before proceeding further.

A mix of Brown Madder and a little Neutral Tint was used for the darker shadow areas in the trees, and a rigger, with the same, but stronger colours gave me the trunks and branches. I softened some of the branches with a damp brush carrying no colour.

The foreground needed to be subtle, and a series of washes of Cadmium Orange and Raw Sienna gave the dry grass effect. The shadows came out of Light Red and Neutral Tint. Then I used my rigger carrying a mix of Light Red, Madder Brown and Neutral Tint for the pathway and darker tones in the bottom left corner.

* I find that a landscape tends to work better if the foreground area takes up no more than one-third of the painting.

Autumn Woodland

Detail of the boats.

Boats at Maryport, Cumbria

One usually associates the Lake District with all those wonderful hills, lakes and skies. But, out on the west coast there are busy harbours with an abundance of boats – sitting there waiting to be painted. One such harbour is at Maryport, just a short drive from my usual course base at Higham Hall near Keswick. There were fifteen of us here, a hazy mist adding mystery to the subject and, after my demonstration most of us completed a scene similar to the one shown here.

I used a size ten round sable, my rigger and Whatman 200lb rough surface paper size 11" x 15"

The colours used were:

Naples Yellow, Light Red, Brown Madder, Ultramarine Blue, Burnt Sienna, Raw Sienna and Sap Green. I also used a sponge and a paper stencil to lift out the moon, and a fine drawing black pen for the rigging on the boats.

I dampened the *whole* paper with clean water and ran Naples Yellow over the whole area. While *still* wet I added a thin wash of Light Red and followed that, *still wet*, with a mix of Ultramarine Blue and Brown Madder. I kept that last mix away from the light area in the sky by tilting my board. I allowed this all to dry before proceeding further.

Next came the distant hills, again with a mix of Brown Madder and Ultramarine Blue. I softened the top of the hills by pushing the colour in towards the hills, with a clean finger.

The largest of the boats came next. Ensuring that this boat was not too central, I painted the overall shape with a thin wash of Burnt Sienna. While still damp, I added Raw Sienna on the right side, thin Sap Green on the left side and then Brown Madder along the top. A touch of Neutral Tint was then used for the subtle shadows. The mast was made from Neutral tint and Brown Madder – with the Rigger brush.

Ultramarine Blue with Neutral Tint made the blue/grey boats, the brown boats were a combination of Light Red with a touch of Neutral Tint. Neat Neutral Tint was used on all the shadows around the boats, and the rigging and ropes were drawn using a black drawing pen.

The foreground texture on the shore was Burnt Sienna with Sap Green dropped in to suggest seaweed.

 Finally, I lifted out the moon with a stencil – a circle the size of a one pence piece cut out of paper, using a small damp sponge.

* Did you know that Naples Yellow will not make green when mixed with blue? Useful when dropping sunshine into a blue sky.

Boats at Maryport, Cumbria

Detail.

Plaza Meyor, Castellor, Spain

One of the most fascinating courses that I recall having tutored was on the Spanish mainland, quite near Gibraltar, in 1996. Having several different nationalities on this painting holiday, greatly added to the interest of travelling around this part of Andalucia . On one of our trips into the Andalucian hills we found this lovely old castle. It was of course the archway that attracted us to this subject. I painted it as a demonstration, with my fellow painters and several locals looking on.

I used a size ten sable throughout on 300lb Saunders Waterford rough paper 11" x 15".

The colours used were:

Raw Sienna, Burnt Sienna,, Light Red. Neutral Tint, Burnt Umber and Sap Green.
I also used a drawing pen for fine line work, which was added when the painting was completed.

I sketched in the positions of the main objects with a 2b pencil and commenced the painting, using a mix of Raw Sienna and Burnt Sienna for the building surrounding the arch. The brickwork of the arch came next with mainly Light Red and just a touch of Raw Sienna on the lighter tones. The bricks on the back of the arch consisted of Burnt and Raw Sienna. A mixture of Burnt Sienna and Neutral Tint made the shadow inside the arch. The lamp above was mainly Neutral Tint with Burnt Sienna for the light bulb.

The closed doorway on the left was also just Neutral Tint, with the suggestion of the brickwork at the base made with Light Red, Raw and Burnt Sienna. The wall on the right came next with a weak wash of Light Red and Neutral Tint. The shadows on the building, under the arch and on the wall were added when dry with Neutral Tint, Light red and Raw Sienna.

The little "Cameo landscape" through the arch was just indicated – no real detail. Cobalt Blue on the sky, Sap Green with Raw Sienna on the hills and bushes, and Light Red on the two rooftops.

The foreground has been suggested with washes of Light Red, Neutral Tint and weak Sap Green on the grasses. I then used the black drawing pen to emphasise the dark cracks on the brickwork paving stones.

The work was then completed. (Approximate painting time – thirty- five minutes).

* Using a rough surface paper helps to give texture when painting buildings.

Plaza Meyor, Castellor. Spain. '96

Bryan A. Thatcher

Plaza Meyor, Castellor, Spain

Early morning mist.

Mist on Bassenthwaite Lake

Early morning mist is quite common in Cumbria and of course it does add something to a painting if one is able to capture it. There is no secret to depicting this atmosphere, one simply requires a limited palette and the use of soft subdued colours. I painted this subject in September 1999 as a demonstration, by the side of the lake. No initial drawing was required and the painting took about thirty minutes.

Colours used were:

Naples Yellow, Neutral Tint, Brown Madder, Cobalt Blue and Raw Sienna.

My flat wash brush and a size ten round sable were the only brushes used, on Saunders Waterford 300lb rough surface paper size 11" x 15."

I commenced by wetting the whole area above the lake with Naples Yellow. While this was still wet I introduced a wash of Neutral Tint from each top corner and tilted my board to allow this colour to run away from the central light. I then allowed the sky to dry completely.

Before painting the hills with a mix of Neutral Tint and Cobalt Blue, I dampened the area on the left - hand hill, where I required the mist to drop over the edge of the hill. That moisture softened the edge of the hill as I painted. The hill on the right side was added and I pushed the colour back from the centre with a clean tissue.

While the hill was still damp, I suggested the trees with Brown Madder mixed with Neutral Tint, and also added Raw Sienna at the base of the hills to suggest a grass bank. When this was dry, I indicated the tree trunks with Neutral Tint mixed with Brown Madder.

I painted the lake using the same colours as the sky, plus a weak Brown Madder, ensuring that the Naples Yellow in the lake reflected below the Naples Yellow in the sky.

A shade stronger touch of Neutral Tint was used in the bottom left foreground, and when that was dry a stronger Neutral Tint suggested the darks.

* A touch of warmth in the foreground will always help to bring the area forward.

Mist on Bassenthwaite Lake

Calf Close Bay, Detail.

Roses for my Mother

I painted this delightful little subject for my mother some years ago and it remains one of my own favourites. When painting flowers, I prefer to have a few blooms lying on my work- top. I invent the composition and arrangement as I work. For some artists the background to flower paintings present a problem. I keep my backgrounds simple by just adding washes around the subjects when the remainder of the painting is complete.

I used a size twelve round sable throughout, on Whatman 200lb rough paper size 10" x 8"

Colours used were:

Cadmium Yellow Deep, Cadmium Orange, Raw Sienna, Ultramarine Blue and Brown Madder.

Looking for a loose, free result here, I decided to use a larger size twelve round sable. I started by mixing Cadmium Yellow Deep with a little Cadmium Orange, and used this to suggest the shapes of the three blooms. I left some white of the paper to give me a few highlights.

When the painting was just damp I strengthened the blooms with more of the same mix. The foliage greens were made out of Cadmium Yellow Deep and Ultramarine Blue. These were painted very loosely and while they were still damp, I added the shadows with a wash of Ultramarine Blue and Brown Madder.

The background came next. I dampened the whole of the background area with clean water and dropped in Raw Sienna, followed by a weak solution of Light Red and finally added a little more Ultramarine and Brown Madder in the area closer to, and behind the blooms.

* If you have problems controlling all that fiddlling, why not try using a larger brush?

Roses for My Mother

Detail.

Winter Rules

The Course was closed at my golf club. No golf! So I took a few photographs (too cold to sketch) and later painted this in my studio. It is really just a colour sketch, but it is nice and fresh with translucent colours.

The colours used were:

Cobalt Blue, Brown Madder, Light Red, Raw Sienna, Sap Green, Burnt Umber and Neutral Tint.

Brushes used were:

My flat wash brush, size ten round sable and a Rigger. Paper was Whatman 200lb rough surface paper Size 8" x 10"

With my wash brush I covered the sky area with a wash of Raw Sienna mixed with Light Red. While still wet, I ran a mix of Brown Madder and Cobalt Blue into the two top corners before lifting out the clouds with a clean dry tissue. I added a stronger mix of Raw Sienna and Light Red to the undersides of the clouds.

While the sky was still damp, I suggested the distant hill and some of the trees on the left with more of the Brown Madder and Cobalt Blue mixture. I then painted the trees with Raw Sienna mixed with Sap Green and Neutral Tint. These were painted very loosely with very little indication of any detail. Burnt Umber was added to suggest the shadows under the trees.

Leaving the white of the paper for most of the foreground snow, the shadows were made from Cobalt Blue and Neutral Tint, with just a touch of Brown Madder on the warmer shadows. The flagpole was indicated with Neutral Tint using my rigger, and the flag itself with clean Brown Madder.

* If you are tempted to paint outside in the cold winter, do not forget that flask of tea, or even something stronger!

Winter Rules !

"Winter Rules"

Detail.

Borth-y-Gest, Snowdonia

I tutored a long weekend watercolour course in North Wales, and we were based quite near Snowdon. This was during October and unfortunately the weather was not kind to us. In fact, this painting was the only one we were able to produce in situ. I demonstrated this subject between the showers at Borth-y-Gest, a mile or so from Port Maddock.

I used my flat wash brush, a size ten round sable and my rigger on Saunders Waterford 300lb rough surface paper, size 11" x 15"

The colours used here are:

Ultramarine Blue, Brown Madder, Raw Sienna, Burnt Sienna, Cobalt Blue and Neutral Tint.

The sky was dampened with clean water and I ran a mix of Cobalt Blue and Brown Madder through the moisture, tipping the board at an angle so that some of the sky remained white. While the sky was still damp, I added the distant hill on the right with the same mix as the sky – but with a shade more Brown Madder. I then allowed the painting to dry.

The main hill was laid in with a stronger mix of the same two colours. While still damp, I added Raw Sienna to make the green. I softened the right hand edge of the hill with a clean dry tissue.

A thin mix of Raw and Burnt Sienna was used for the far sandy area, and the water was made with Cobalt Blue and Neutral Tint. The smaller red boats are Brown Madder and the larger boats were alternatively, Neutral Tint, Ultramarine Blue, a mix of Brown Madder and then Neutral Tint. Detail and the masts on the boats were added with Neutral Tint using my rigger.

The foreground sand was again a mix of the two Siennas, and the suggestions of seaweed were made with a mix of Ultramarine Blue and Raw Sienna. The rocks and the darks were various strengths of Neutral tint on my rigger.

* When painting a subject that includes boats and distant hills, you may find that it helps the composition if the masts break the line of the hills.

Borth-y-Gest, Snowdonia

Chicago skyline, Detail.

Chicago Skyline

This painting started out as a pencil sketch, progressed to a watercolour and finished up as a Line and Wash! I completed it during a most enjoyable trip to the USA, to paint Lake Michigan and it's surrounding landscapes, also to exhibit my work of the English Lake District. I travelled the length of Michigan, which I found was not dissimilar to Cumbria in the UK, particularly at the North. My exhibition was a complete sell out, the Americans were very welcoming and I look forward to returning there in the not too distant future.

I used a 2b pencil, an Edding drawing pen and a size ten round sable. Saunders Waterford 300lb Not surface paper, size 11" x 15" was used.

Colours for this composition were:

Cobalt Blue, Light Red, Brown Madder, Raw Sienna, Sap Green and Neutral Tint.

A 2b pencil sketch gave me the outlines of the buildings, before suggesting the sky with Cobalt Blue, a touch of Brown Madder and just a little Raw Sienna and Light Red to add colour on the left.

I then realised that this was going to work better as a Line and Wash, so proceeded with my Edding drawing pen (Size 5) to make the buildings and detail more prominent. I tried not to include too much detail and used broken lines throughout the drawing. For example, no windows were drawn, just indicated, as were the tree trunks and shoreline.

When the drawing was complete I dropped the colour on the buildings, noting that the light was coming from the left, and therefore the shadows would fall on the right hand side of the buildings and the trees. The warmer light tones were made from Raw Sienna and Light Red, and the heavier warm tones made from Brown Madder and Cobalt Blue. The cooler buildings were made from a mix of Cobalt Blue, Brown Madder and Neutral Tint.

The trees were a mixture of Sap Green and a little Raw Sienna. Light Red and Raw Sienna indicated the shoreline. Lake Michigan is a mix of varying tones including Cobalt Blue and Brown Madder.

* A drawing pen can be quite useful – but make sure you are aware of it being either waterproof or water soluble. I use waterproof pens.

Chicago Skyline 1986

Bryan A. Thatcher

Chicago Skyline

Detail.

Lake Michigan, USA

Here is another subject, painted on one of my trips to the USA. It is always nice to return home from a journey with a few paintings rather than a roll of film. Paintings have a more personal feel and they are a good reminder of the challenge experienced. This subject was painted early one morning in October and the colours of the landscape really suited my palette.

Brushes: Size ten round sable, rigger and my flat wash brush. Paper: Whatman 200lb rough surface size 8" x 10"

Colours: Naples Yellow, Light Red, Ultramarine Blue, Brown Madder, Raw Sienna, Burnt Sienna and Neutral Tint.

I dampened the whole of the sky area with clean water and then, with my flat wash brush, first added Naples Yellow then Light Red and finally a mix of Ultramarine and Brown Madder. I allowed these colours to flow through the moisture, tilting my board to keep the final wash away from the light in the centre. More of the final wash was added in the bottom left to indicate the distant hills.

When the sky was completely dry, a strong mix of Ultramarine and Brown Madder gave me the under-colour of the two main hills. When just damp, I introduced a strong mix of Prussian Blue and Burnt Sienna which I laid over the under-colour, allowing some of that under-colour to show through. My rigger was then used to indicate the tops of the silhouetted trees, pushing out the wet colour with the point of the brush. Note how some whites of the paper have been left at the base of the hills.

I then repeated the sky colours in the foreground water, ensuring that this was darker at the base, and very importantly, the lake was left white on the horizon. This helped the contrast, which I wanted to be dramatic. The foreground was painted while dry, with a fairly dry brush. Using the side of the brush on the rough surface paper helped to leave a few white lights. Quite a useful technique.

The painting was completed, when the foreground was dry, by introducing Burnt Sienna on the shallow water and also indicating the dark rocks with a strong Neutral Tint in my Rigger.

* I find it helpful to have a spare strip of watercolour paper available to try mixed colours, before committing them to the painting.

Lake Michigan, USA

Tarn Valley, Detail.

The Tarn Valley, South of France

This was painted as a demonstration while tutoring a watercolour course, near Toulouse in the South of France – at breakfast time! I recall students having their meal while I was enjoying painting this lovely quiet landscape. There were several nationalities on this course and the Europeans could all speak English. But the students from England ? Yes, we struggled!

I used my flat wash brush, a size ten round sable and a rigger on Whatman 200lb rough surface paper, size 8" x 10"

Colours used were:

Cobalt Blue, Neutral Tint, Ultramarine Blue, Brown Madder, Light Red, Cadmium Yellow Deep and Raw Sienna.

I dampened the whole of the sky area with clean water and ran Cobalt Blue through the moisture. Then Neutral Tint was added for the cloud shadows. I waited until the sky was just damp and then lifted out the white clouds with a clean tissue.

When completely dry, I indicated the distant hills with a mix of Ultramarine Blue and Brown Madder. I then lifted some of this colour off the hills, again using a tissue.

All the greens in this watercolour painting were made out of varying strengths of a mix consisting of Ultramarine and Raw Sienna. Some of these were warmed slightly with the addition of a little Brown Madder. The darker tones were painted with my rigger.

The cornfields, (the colour of which made the whole subject easier on the eye), were painted with differing tones and mixes of Cadmium Yellow Deep and Light Red. One or two areas of white paper have been left unpainted in the landscape and these help to give more contrast. The dry grasses on the bottom left were added with my rigger, using a mix of Light Red and Neutral Tint.

* Try to use "Artistic Licence" whenever the opportunity arises. Our aim is to turn the subject into a painting – not a photograph.

Damiette, France '94

Bryan A. Thatcher.

The Tarn Valley, South of France

Detail.

Winter Trees

This is a very loose watercolour painting taken from a pencil sketch in my studio. The side of the large rigger brush has been used extensively. This helps to restrict fiddling with any detail. The only suggestion of detail was made with the point of rigger brush, which was very helpful adding the darker branches on the trees and reeds.

I used a size fourteen round sable and a rigger on Saunders Waterford 300lb rough surface paper.
Size 15" x 11".

Colours: Cobalt Blue, Brown Madder, Burnt Sienna, Raw Sienna, Burnt Umber, Neutral Tint, Ceruleum Blue and Cadmium Yellow Deep.

The sky was a weak mixture of Cobalt Blue and Brown Madder. Some of the area was left white to show the soft cloud – the edges were softened with paper tissue. The distant trees were indicated with a stronger mix of the same two colours and the less distant trees with an even stronger mix.

The grass bank under those trees was a mixture of Cadmium Yellow Deep and Raw Sienna. Then the sky colours were added to the foreground.

The trees in the top left area were painted with the side of my round sable. Firstly, with a mix of Cobalt Blue, Ceruleum Blue and Neutral Tint. Then I dropped in Burnt Umber and Neutral Tint to give the lower darker shadow areas. While still damp, I suggested the under colour of the reeds with a mix of Burnt Sienna and Raw Sienna. The stronger reeds were added with a rigger, using the same two colours, when the under colour was dry.

The trees on the right were painted in the same way, using the same colours but without the use of Ceruleum at the top.

The painting was completed by the introduction of the darker branches, using strong Neutral Tint. A weaker Neutral tint on the shadows of the water was added, and finally the reeds in the bottom right foreground came with Burnt Sienna and one or two darker ones with Neutral Tint.

* If you try using a larger brush, but feel uncomfortable with it, don't give up. Persevere for a while, and it will help to loosen up your work.

Winter Trees

Detail.

Pines in Perthshire

Painted in Scotland while tutoring near Perth, this is quite a satisfying result. Nice and loose, no real detail – all trees are just free brushstrokes that somehow seemed to work. The colourful sky is my "artistic licence" at work. Again, the greens are mixed out of yellows, blues and browns, no manufacturers greens used at all.

Brushes used: Flat wash brush and a size ten sable, on Whatman 200lb rough surface paper. Size 11" x 15"

Colours used: Naples Yellow, Light Red, Brown Madder, Ultramarine Blue, Prussian Blue, Burnt Sienna, Burnt Umber, Raw Sienna, Cadmium Yellow Deep and Neutral Tint.

Using my wash brush, I dampened the whole of the sky area with a weak mix of Naples Yellow and Light Red. While still fairly wet, I added a mix of Ultramarine Blue and Brown Madder, tilting the board to let this mix run away from the central light area. The distant hills were added when the sky was dry, with just a touch of Neutral Tint. The not- so - distant trees were a mixture of Ultramarine and Neutral Tint.

The pine trees were a mix of Burnt Sienna and Prussian Blue and also Burnt Umber and Prussian Blue. A touch of Neutral Tint was dropped into the trees where darker tones were required. Best not to fiddle with these trees – if the brush strokes are left alone as you lay the colour they will remain free and loose. Note how lights have been left within the tree shapes.

The grass bank was made from an original wash of Raw Sienna and Ultramarine Blue, then a touch of Cadmium Yellow Deep was added while still wet. I allowed this to dampen and then added the shadows under the trees.

Finally, the water in the foreground came from repeating the sky colours, and while still wet, I added the green tree reflections in the water by again mixing Burnt Sienna with Prussian Blue.

* The sky will very often take up to at least half of a landscape painting, sometimes more. It is therefore a good idea to ensure that the sky is interesting.

Pines in Perthshire

Detail.

Bluebell Wood

This is a small fresh watercolour, which I first painted as a tutorial on one of my series of video tapes. I recall it well because it was completed in less than ten minutes! We were timing the filming of the tape and were quite amazed. Other demonstrations on this particular videotape took longer and we were able to include four subjects. Nevertheless, this subject has proven to be a good exercise in setting a target for painting time. See how you get on.

Brushes: Size ten round sable and my rigger. On Whatman 200lb rough surface paper, size 8" x 10"

Colours: Cadmium Yellow Deep, Ultramarine Blue, Burnt Umber, Neutral Tint, Burnt Sienna and Windsor Violet.

No drawing was required here. I started the effect of the woodland tree foliage by mixing Cadmium Yellow Deep with Ultramarine Blue. Using the side of the brush, which was not too wet, I laid the colour down allowing the rough surface of the paper to give me the "bird holes." I carried this down to around two thirds of the paper. I then dropped in more Cadmium Yellow Deep to show the lighter areas in the foliage. The darker tones of the foliage were indicated with the original mix, plus a touch of Burnt Umber, and again the colour on my brush was not too wet.

The tree trunks were painted with my rigger carrying Burnt Umber and Neutral Tint. The branches were made from the same mix and I painted most of these in the "bird holes."

A very weak wash of Windsor Violet was laid on the areas where I wished the bluebells to be. When this was completely dry, I used a much stronger Ultramarine Blue, using the side of my rigger, to give the suggestion of bluebell detail. This effect is known as "scrumbling."

The pathway was made with Burnt Sienna, ensuring that the path had an interesting curve. The shadows on the path were indicated with a weak Neutral Tint. I then used a mix of Cadmium Yellow Deep, Ultramarine Blue and Neutral Tint to make the green grass in the foreground surrounding the bluebells. Some of this colour mix was also dropped into the bluebells to give a softer "Wet-into- Wet" appearance.

* It can be an interesting exercise to set a limited time to complete a small watercolour. Best to mix all your colours before commencing.

Bluebell Wood

Detail.

Aldeburgh, Suffolk

This was painted on the beach at Aldeburgh during a very pleasant weekend, which my wife and I spent in this part of Suffolk in August 1999. I had recently tutored a watercolour course at Snape Maltings and enjoyed it so much, that I decided it would be nice to return while the summer months were still with us.

There was nothing too demanding about this subject, but as a watercolour sketch it has possibilities as a reference for a more serious work. I used a fairly large sheet size here, which always allows the use of larger brushes, and consequently paint more loosely.

Brushes: Size fourteen round sable and a rigger, on Whatman 200lb rough surface paper, size 20" x 16"

Colours: Cobalt Blue, Ultramarine Blue, Brown Madder, Burnt Sienna, Raw Sienna and Neutral Tint.

The sky was just Cobalt blue brushed on with my large round sable. I used the side of the brush to push the colour around, leaving soft edges on the lighter cloud areas. I allowed this to dry completely before adding the birds with my rigger using Neutral Tint.

The whole of the buildings and the distant shapes were painted with a mixture of Ultramarine and Brown Madder. I left a few whites of the paper to suggest detail – windows etc. At this stage I added the water using Cobalt Blue with just a touch of Neutral Tint.

I had previously left whites in the "busy" central area. This was then used for the boats, which I was able to make by adding detail around the whites. For this I used touches of Brown Madder, Cobalt Blue and Neutral Tint. The masts were added with my rigger, using a dark tone made with Neutral Tint and Brown Madder.

Burnt Sienna mixed with Raw Sienna made up the foreground. (I omitted the many stones on the beach). Finally, I touched a weak mix of Neutral Tint and Ultramarine Blue into the water on the right hand side, then added the figures, using mostly Burnt Sienna on the bodies, Brown Madder for the red figures and Neutral Tint on the heads of the bathers in the water.

* Brown Madder, in its neat clean form, is actually a beautiful strong red – almost a "Poppy Red."

Aldeburgh, Suffolk

72

Detail.

Poppy Fields, Oxfordshire

The green fields of England are greatly enhanced when poppies appear – and who can resist painting them? A good loose result is possible if we see the blooms as groups of colour, rather than individual flowers. After all, these flowers usually grow in groups. There is nothing so lonely as a single poppy, especially in a field. This particular field is in Ewelme, a few miles from Oxford.

Brushes: Size ten round sable and my large flat wash brush, on Whatman 200lb rough surface paper, size 11" x 15"

Colours: Naples Yellow, Light Red, Ultramarine Blue, Brown Madder, Neutral Tint, Burnt Sienna, Raw Sienna and Prussian Blue.

The sky was moistened with clean water before I added separate washes of Naples Yellow, Light Red and a mix of Ultramarine Blue and Brown Madder. I tilted my board to allow the last wash to run away from the lighter area. The sky needed to dry completely before proceeding further.

The distant trees and bushes were made with a mixture of Neutral Tint and Ultramarine Blue. I added Raw Sienna to the trees on the left to indicate a hazy green/grey. Neutral Tint made the darks on those trees and also the suggestion of the small fence.

The whole of the foreground was washed over with a weak mixture of Raw Sienna and just a touch of Prussian Blue – leaving a few whites as highlights to add interest. While this was still damp, I added a stronger mixture of Raw Sienna and Prussian Blue to make the stronger tones of green. I then added Burnt Sienna under the trees, left and right, which gave the painting a little more warmth.

Clean Brown Madder was the red used for the suggestion of poppies.

The composition was helped by the suggestion of a slope from left to right. I felt that without the slope, the overall appearance was too horizontal.

* Just a reminder. When painting into a damp area, do make sure that the colour you are inserting is no wetter than the damp colour you are painting into.

Poppy Fields, Oxfordshire

Detail.

Grange Bridge, Borrowdale

I have painted this bridge many times – and find something different on each occasion! This painting has been given quite a bit of "artistic licence." There is actually a group of trees between each span of the bridge, I have given more warmth to the colour of the bridge, and the hills are even more dominant than they appear here. Nevertheless, I am quite satisfied with this result, which was painted as a demonstration during a tutoring course at nearby Higham Hall.

Brushes: Size ten round sable and my rigger, on Whatman 200lb rough surface paper size 11" x 15"

Colours: Cobalt Blue, Light Red, Naples Yellow, Raw Sienna, Burnt Sienna, Ultramarine Blue and Neutral Tint.

I sketched in the shape of the bridge and small buildings before laying the sky wash down to, and above the drawing. Naples Yellow first, then weak Light Red, followed by weak Cobalt Blue. I allowed this to dry completely. The hills came next, with a mixture of Light Red and Raw Sienna, which was painted down to the top of the bridge. While still damp, I added the trees using varying mixes of Cadmium Yellow Deep and Ultramarine Blue, being careful to paint around the rooftops.

The bridge itself came next. Firstly, by laying a thin wash of Burnt Sienna over the whole structure, then glazing each end with Neutral Tint. When this was dry I added the texture with a touch stronger Burnt Sienna, using my rigger. Raw Sienna was used to add colour under the bridge and allowed to dry before placing in the darks under the two spans with Neutral Tint. I also added colour to the buildings with the rigger, mixing Ultramarine Blue and Neutral Tint. The telegraph poles and chimney pots were just Neutral Tint – quite strong.

The water in the River Derwent was painted using the sky colours, which I allowed to dry before adding the horizontal suggestions of shadows and rocks on the water. Neutral Tint for the darker tones and a mix of weak Neutral Tint and stronger Ultramarine Blue on the others.

The painting was completed by introducing the grass banks, and for these I used an initial weak wash of Raw Sienna and Ultramarine Blue. After this, the darker greens were added using a fairly strong mix of Cadmium Yellow Deep and Ultramarine Blue.

* It can be quite helpful to paint larger areas with the side of your brush. This helps to spread the colour more quickly and loosely.

Grange Bridge, Cumbria

Bryan A. Thatcher

Grange Bridge, Borrowdale

Detail.

Rosas, Spain

This is another simple loose watercolour that can be painted quite quickly. It will help if colours are mixed before proceeding and also if a little time is spent observing and planning the composition. My wife and I spent our honeymoon in Rosas, so I have a special affection for this painting.

Brushes: Size fourteen round sable and my rigger. Saunders Waterford 300lb rough surface paper was used. Size 11" x 15"

Colours: Ultramarine Blue, Brown Madder, Light Red, Burnt Sienna, Raw Sienna, Ceruleum Blue and Neutral Tint.

I dampened the sky area with clean water and ran a weak mix of Ultramarine Blue and Brown Madder into the top, allowing this to run through the moisture. I tilted my board to allow the wash to run away from the lighter areas. While this was still wet, I dropped into each top corner a very weak Light Red, again tilting my board. I then allowed the sky to dry.

The distant hills (The Pyrenees) were a stronger mix of the Ultramarine Blue and Brown Madder. The dark trees on the left were an even stronger mix of the same two colours – but I added Raw Sienna while the tone was still damp, to give the dark green effect.

The colour of the Mediterranean Sea, (which does not always reflect the sky colour) was made with Ceruleum Blue – leaving some dry horizontal whites of the paper, to add interest.

I used a mix of Raw and Burnt Sienna for the foreground, and also on the sides of the cliffs. Suggestions of detail were added to the bottom of the cliffs and distant hills with my rigger, using a touch of Neutral Tint.

Finally, and most importantly, came the reeds and foliage in the right foreground. These balanced the composition. I again used the strong mixture of Ultramarine Blue and Brown Madder before dropping Raw Sienna in to give a suggestion of dark green. The reeds were painted with my Rigger.

* This is a simple result that one could try with a time limit. Aim for twenty minutes, but remember to mix your colours before proceeding.

Rosas, Spain

Detail.

Playa Rocha, Portugal

We have spent several holidays on the Algarve in Portugal. My wife loves the sun and I have similar feelings for golf – so we were both satisfied! Of course, my watercolours travel with me and who could resist at least some of the interesting rocky coastline? This type of subject calls for a great deal of planning, and it is sometimes necessary to view several aspects before settling down. It was certainly the case for this piece of work. I got there eventually, but I am not too sure if I gave the subject the result it deserved!

Brushes : Just one size ten round sable on Saunders Waterford 300lb rough surface paper, size 8" x 10"

Colours: Naples Yellow, Raw Sienna, Burnt Sienna, Cobalt Blue, Light Red, Neutral Tint and Burnt Umber.

Although pure blue in reality, I decided on a warmer, more subtle sky. Cobalt Blue at the top, weak Light Red through the centre and just a touch of Naples Yellow down to the horizon. I then allowed this to dry, (in fact it dried almost as I painted) before using a 2b pencil to softly indicate the position of the rock formations. I tend not to do too much drawing, as this has a tendency to tighten up my work when adding colours.

The distant cliff tops were a mix of Cobalt Blue and Neutral Tint – a little weaker in tone for the furthest cliffs. I then laid a mixed wash of Raw Sienna, Burnt Sienna and just a little Light Red over the three main rock formations. When dry, I added the softer shadows with Raw Sienna, Burnt Umber and Cobalt Blue. I softened the edges of these colours with a clean damp brush carrying a little clean water. The darker tones were then painted using Neutral Tint and Burnt Umber.

The water came next, for which I used the sky colours, plus a touch of Neutral Tint in the Cobalt Blue. Note that the brush strokes of the nearer water are running at an angle to indicate quiet rollers moving toward the beach. The foreground beach was made from Raw Sienna and Burnt Sienna and the light shadows on the sand were added with a glaze of Neutral Tint and Cobalt Blue

Finally, the darker rocks on the beach and in the water were added, with strong mixes of Neutral Tint and Burnt Umber. Weak Burnt Sienna made the lights on these rocks.

Playa Rocha, Portugal

Detail.

Crummockwater, Cumbria

This is a lake which I visit two or three times a year when tutoring at Higham Hall in the Lake District, so I should know it well! But Crummockwater has a dual personality. Seen here in this watercolour painting it is quiet and serene- the lake itself is still and like glass, with motionless reflections. On other occasions a strong wind can send rollers towards the shore at an alarming rate. When calm though, it is the quietest place, just right for a "painting picnic."

Brushes: Size fourteen round sable on Saunders Waterford 300lb rough surface paper, size 11" x 15"

Colours: Cobalt Blue, Neutral Tint, Prussian Blue, Light Red, Raw Sienna, Brown Madder, Burnt Umber, Ultramarine Blue and Cadmium Yellow Deep.

I used no pencil drawing for this composition and just the one brush. The sky was painted on dry paper with various strengths of Cobalt Blue mixed with a little Neutral Tint. Some of the clouds were left white, others lifted out with a clean tissue. When dry, the distant hills were painted with the same mix.

The central hill came first with Light Red used for the left side, Raw Sienna in the centre and Burnt Umber on its right hand side. The hill on the left was made with a mix of Ultramarine Blue, Brown Madder and Burnt Umber. The trees were added while the hill was still damp, using Sap Green, Cadmium Yellow Deep, and then more Burnt Umber at the base of the hill. The hill on the right was mainly Burnt Umber added to Cobalt Blue and then glazed with Raw Sienna.

The water was firstly laid down with a wash of the sky colours – Cobalt Blue and a little Neutral Tint, being careful to leave the horizontal reflections. The reflections of the hills were added, when those colours were completely dry, with a repeat of the mixed colours used on the hills.

Finally, and quite importantly to the composition, came the overhanging tree. Burnt Umber and Prussian Blue made the darker tones, Raw Sienna was introduced, on wet colour, to give the lighter tones of the foliage.

* When you think that a painting on which you are working is almost finished, leave it for a few minutes. Then take a second look – it is probably OK.

Crummock Water, Cumbria.

Bryan A. Thatcher

Crummockwater, Cumbria

Detail.

Sussex Landscape

There are many wonderful landscapes to be painted in the county of Sussex. I tutor watercolour courses at the Old Rectory in Fittleworth, quite close to Pulborough and just a few miles from the coast. This watercolour was painted in the early autumn, and the grass had been scorched by the hot summer sun. The warm colour of the grass made a nice combination with the blue/grey hazy sky, ideal to paint as a demonstration.

Brushes: Size fourteen round sable, flat wash brush and a rigger. Paper was Saunders Waterford 300lb rough surface size 22" x 30"

Colours: Ultramarine Blue, Brown Madder, Light Red, Prussian Blue, Burnt Sienna, Burnt Umber and Neutral Tint.

I used my flat wash brush to paint this sky using Ultramarine Blue with just a touch of Brown Madder on dry paper. When this was dry I used the same mix on the distant hills.

The roof of the cottage and outhouses were made with Light Red using the round sable, and the shadows were added with Neutral Tint while the Light Red was still damp.

The deeper tones on the trees were a mix of Burnt Umber and Prussian Blue. The lighter tones of green were a mix of Burnt Sienna and Prussian Blue. Raw Sienna was added to that mix to make the small bushes.

Before proceeding with the foreground grass, I used my rigger to indicate the chimney pots, telegraph pole and fencing with a strong mix of Burnt Umber and Neutral Tint.

The foreground grass was a mix of Burnt and Raw Sienna. The pathway was a weak mix of Neutral Tint with just a hint of Light Red added. While the grass was still damp I indicated the cloud shadows in the foreground with a touch of Neutral Tint. The same mix was used on the slightly deeper tones on the path.

* If your landscape foregrounds seem too quiet, try a few cloud shadows - before overworking it with clumps of grass etc.

Sussex Landscape

Venice

Venice

Who can resist painting here? I have also painted this in oils and that is somewhere in the USA. This watercolour hangs at home.
Not for sale!

My Gallery

Puerto Banus, Spain

Marigolds.

Made mostly from the Cadmiums, Yellow, Red and Orange.

Light in the Landscape

This is a subject that I have used as a demonstration on many occasions. This is the original, one of my favourites and hangs at home.

Derwentwater, Cumbria.

Sunrise at Derwentwater. One has to get there early to see this wonderful subject.

Venice

A pen drawing with loose washes of watercolour.

Near Loch Lomond
Nice and fresh, and those greens are OK.

Skiddaw. Cumbria

Skiddaw from Bassenthwaite.

This was my first painting completed in the Lake District and hangs at home in our lounge.

Forsythia

My Gallery

Down the Slope

This is one that was definitely not painted in situ!

Dungarpur, Rajasthan

I painted this as a commission for Dr. Hans and Mrs Paru Patel and it is shown here with their kind permission.

My Gallery

Salmon Pink Roses.